WRITINGS IN CHINA

Lewis Codington

MY PURPOSE

Lord, keep me burdened to share your precious, precious Message with those who have never encountered it, met a believer, or visited a fellowship.
7-2011

REMEMBER?

Teenagers we were when we first met.
Remember?
You in your overalls - me in my tan jacket.
I liked your enthusiasm and energy for life;
Your innocent ebullience - and your commitment to God.
Saint Barnabas, the RP, and Doctrine class...
They were better cause you were there.
Then one day it just seemed like the right thing to do
-
To make a lifelong commitment.
Remember?
Soon we were counting honeymoons.
Saint Simons and Washington and Idle Hours.
I loved traveling together -
To Europe and Asia and then to California.
Fun it was to plan our trips -
And to see how far we could stretch our dollars.
Something very special happened one day.
Remember?
You came home from Oak Ridge...
And announced we were having a boy!
And we sure did.
Just as we started a life-changing experience at the CBNook.
Amazingly...eight more surprising gifts then followed.
Remember?

First in America, then in France, and finally the last
three in England.
And the years passed.
A lot of water under the bridge.
We experienced a lot of blessings...
Including some pretty hard things.
Remember?
Bookstores started.
Frightening attacks.
A tragic death.
Depression and cancer.
Our parents crossing over.
Kids off to college, one by one.
Now here we are in a far off corner - SSJ.
And I think back to the promise you made me make.
Remember?
65...We've quietly crossed the halfway mark.
Isn't that amazing!
How many more milestones will we see?
I'm thinking back to that long ago pledge we made.
Remember?
And I sure am glad we did.
I love you.
December 16, 2011
33 years

THE LIGHT WENT OUT TODAY

Electric works, gas is on, candles flickering brightly on the dining room table.
But the light went out today.
I'm feeling it in my belly deep down.
The long anticipated day arrived.
Seemed a far off idea before it came.
Something out there that wouldn't really happen.
Then I awoke this morning and held Elsbeth close.
The day had come...
She was leaving us.
Kids' school, meals, last bit of packing...
With her apron on, Elsbeth moved from room to room, from task to task.
And I watched the last hours fall away.
I rolled her bags down the road from our house to the bus.
We sat still on the narrow bench and waited.
Then it was time.
The clock on the wall showed 11:30.
We got up, walked outside, and watched for the bus to Kunming.
The blue bus pulled up, and I felt my heart sink down.
One last kiss, she climbed the stairs, and the bus swung back into the traffic.
Not even one last glimpse.
The bus was gone, and I shuffled up the cobblestone walkway toward home - alone.

She was gone. Elsbeth had left us.

It will be 27 days till I see her face again, DV.

You see, Elsbeth left today to meet her 10 month grandson for the first time in Nashville.

She's gone. The house seems cold. Skies a little more gray.

For me, the light went out today.

January 19, 2012

OUR CHINA

Dark jagged mountains
Cobblestone walkways
Peppers and spice
The number 2 for a kuai
Cold mountain streams
Brilliant stars on dark nights
Mahjong and cards
Loaded down beilas
Jack's and 88
Hiking the SSJ construction site
Spectacular view from DU
Kay buh kah
Women bent under loads on their way to the market
Cai Cun and Er Hai
Finding B. and Sleepy F.
The Pack and Jakes and heads bright red
Hong Long and Foreigners
Tired, crazy music on Fuxing
Xia Che!
Driving a taxi
Walking the Cang Shan
Zee Burn has landed
English club and Michael
Marga, Jeff, Kalo, Marzena, Rachel, Josiah...and Yu Laoshi
Only 49,000 characters to go
Cheap DVDs...free movies
Cheapuh...cheapuh!

Students on Saturday
Pancho and Vice Mom
Nancy and a bus ride
Canaan Books
Tourists on Fuxing
Print Advice? Count out 2500
Scheduling your shower carefully
TP without holes
No heat…no AC
Slipper and dust
Rice with Kuaizi
Els in the kitchen
JH's guitar
Mr. McBride
SiFangJie bags
Lijiang with B.
Ping pong and billiards
Wah Mah
YiuJu and Amazon
Stella's with the Nelsons
Dyed tapestries
Bai costumes
Carpenter Street
Dali Marble
Green Grocery and ice cream
Boai and the Foreign Shop
Short life light bulbs
Carpenter 38
Helly Potah
Kunming rest stops
Carrie knitting

Top Cup with Liz
Chaos and Puffy
Kids taking a rest on the sidewalk
Mingpians
Fireworks and moon cakes...
January 21, 2012

WHY THIS...

Why this pain, sadness, loss?
Why do we allow this to happen to ourselves?
Why do we cause...create so much damage?
Their eyes speak to us...the anger, the bitterness, the confusion.
What will their future be?
Why do we do this to those we love...to those who depend on us...believe in us?
It makes a mockery of what we believe.
It turns our kids' worlds upside down...and then stomps on and crushes them.
What of commitment, truth, righteousness?
It's a killing cancer.
Why do we give it our world...give it free rein to devour and destroy us?
God hates divorce...shouldn't we?
February 3, 2012
JP, Bo F., Jonah H., Michel K., Dawn L., Alice H.

14

It's happening again...as it always does.
My mind is being pulled.
My thoughts and memories are turned to you...
It's not the date that triggers these reflections.
Not on the 14th of April, when Lincoln was shot.
Nor on July 14, when the Bastille swarm started a revolution in France.
And not on September 14, either, when Key saw a star studded banner.
No, it is only now, on this day in February, on the 14th...
That I think of you in this way.
Years and decades we've spent together.
Probably 35 Valentine's Days in all.
And all those years...
You have loved me.
You alone like no other.
With parents gone, siblings scattered, our children on their own.
You alone have been there.
My thoughts travel back across this span.
And there remains one constant.
You.
There were opportunities you had,
Family events you missed,
Cultural challenges and language struggles.
All these because you stayed here for me.
So of course my thoughts are carried to you.

You are in my thoughts, in my memory, in my life.
Because you chose and sacrificed to be.
So my thoughts are again on you.
February 5, 2012
For my wife

PARTY'S OVER...

I told the kids today that the party's over.
For 28 days they've even living on a very long leash.
Maybe no leash at all...
Leisurely, late mornings
Up all hours of the night
Laptop screens glowing in the dark
Trips to town as and when
Pancakes, crepes, cookies and brownies, meals out, a snack or two, smoothies at home
Soccer, basketball, swimming...during school hours
Rook, Authors, Mahjong...as needed
Nice, cool, towering smoothies a few times at our favorite smoothie joint
Movies on school nights (Did I say that??)
Yes, sir...it's been fine...mighty fine.
But as they say, all good things must come to an end.
We are all so relieved and thankful to have Mom back home with us.
But I had to tell the kids...after 28 days...the party's over.
The boss has landed.
February 16, 2012
Dali, China
Elsbeth's return from a visit to Nashville

A REFLECTION

I see things unpleasant…
No, I see ugly realities,
Lived out in the lives of my neighbors
Casting out a blanket of judgment,
That covers those around them
Displaying criticism of those who are different
Choosing to be intolerant
Desiring to avoid those who cost them something
Looking down on others who surely have fewer
talents than do they
Holding tightly to the memory of perceived wrong
done against them
Controlling others to achieve their own agendas
Puzzling at how God could possibly use…or have
even chosen…others to serve him.
How could my neighbors be such a fountain of what
is putrid?
How could they spew such garbage?
Then God pulls open my eye lids…
And shows me that the filth I see comes from me.
All that I've been seeing
Is a reflection of me.
All along I've been looking at and seeing myself
That is what Jesus died for…
This is what needed to be cleaned out.
This is what Jesus did for me.
Lord, keep carving the rotten
Out of my life.

LEWIS CODINGTON

March 13, 2012

SHE IS GRACE

Into my life she came
Unexpected, unsought
An explosion of joy
An innocent, fresh burst of enthusiasm
Sharing her heart, her life, her beliefs
Her love
She poured out grace.
She was beautiful
A beauty that flowed out of her
Beauty that made her radiant
That came from giving to others.
A love was planted and took root
Love that was given fully
Love that wasn't interested in what I lacked
In my wrongs, in my shortcomings
As if she couldn't see anything bad
She kept loving me.
How could she do this, give this?
Keep loving me as no one else.
It's something I don't understand
Something I don't deserve.
But it's beyond how I am or what I do
It is steadfast and keeps on
Unconditional, undeserved, unending.
It is grace.
She is grace.
March 14, 2012
For my wife

WILL WE FORGET?

They come to us
Never having seen
Never having met
Never having entered...
Will we forget?
A homeless bird finding rest
A restless soul seeking peace
A frightened girl burdened by family responsibilities
A shy guy looking for a way forward
A gentle young man, traumatized by tragedy and a load too heavy
One believing in himself, and wanting help to succeed in the West
A sensitive student, feeling beaten by bullying and failure
A beauty who, having grown up alone with parents too busy, longs to be with us
A talented gal who we've poured days and weeks into, bound by teaching and tradition
A quiet, gentle girl, soaking up our conversations, intense in her attention
One who stays and stays and stays...lonely and not wanting to leave our home
A happy, fun-loving guy, interested but wanting primarily to enjoy his life
A girl who is too bad, burdened by her past
A guy who says, "I want to be like you."

Never having seen the Message, met a Family member, entered the House...
They come to us
Privileged we are to have such friends
Will we forget the many others still to encounter?
March 17, 2012

WHO ARE YOU?

Where were you at the beginning?
When was the beginning for you?
How do we understand who you are?
Can we only see glimpses, reflections of you?
Why did David, the man with a heart for you, have such frustration with you?
Why did the good man, Job, perceive you as unfair?
Why was Moses, the meek, so angry at you at times?
Why was wise Solomon...such a fool?
How could Samson, so infused with your power and Spirit, throw so much away?
Lord, who are you?
Will we ever only see glimpses, shadows, hints?
Even all these great believers of yesteryear did not understand.
Lord, to who else can we go?
Lord, you are the way to eternal life.
Help me to believe...even though I don't understand.
March 18, 2012

DALI IN SPRING

Walking along the cobblestone with Davy, heading
toward town
I look up...
Silent explosions above me
Explosions unreal, impossible
Intricate and delicate to the extreme
Too beautiful for my eyes
Explosions of amaranth, carnation, cerise, and
fuchsia
Lavender, magenta, Persian rose
These words...
Beautiful and descriptive in themselves
Fail to express the pink explosion
God has thrown down on our heads
Bursting atop the cherry trees.
Dali in spring...
March 27, 2012

POETRY

In school I hated poetry.
Limericks were OK, but if they wanted to tell me a sunrise was beautiful, why didn't they just say so?
Why all this tap dancing around the point without really getting to it?
A strange thing happened in December...
I started putting some thoughts down on paper that a few have mistaken for poetry.
I've even read a few of these scribbles to several students to challenge their comprehension of English.
Beautiful! Wow! You should publish them in a book!
In this culture, these are the only acceptable responses to something presented by an elder or teacher.
They have to like it...enthusiastically...
Sweet payback for the years I suffered through poetry classes.
March 29, 2012

EAST AND WEST

I flew east and arrived in the West last month.
My friends said I had lost weight.
That surprised me.
What do you eat there, they asked.
We eat rice every day and walk a lot.
They laughed, and a Korean guy, who I thought would be sympathetic, said between chuckles, you must be starving in China!
Several weeks, and not a few bowls of ice cream later, I flew west to return to the East.
I felt pretty good. I had lost weight…it obviously was noticeable.
The students here will have none of it.
Pointing to my belly, they laugh, You're fat!
You have a basketball under your shirt!
Asian respect for elders does not include weight sensitivities.
Such different perspectives.
No wonder East is East and West is West.
March 29, 2012

A WALK

Through the dim remnants of early dawn I see him coming.

A foreign devil approaching through the trees in the distance.

It's obvious he's a foreigner with his tan jacket and baseball cap.

That's OK...I'm a foreigner, too.

But he's a Yankee from MN...that's harder to stomach.

We meet up as a big orange ball lifts itself out of the lake on the eastern horizon.

He hands me a thin plastic bag with a thick round disk of bread in it, nearly an inch thick.

I bite into the warm bread and my teeth sink into the brown bean curd within.

Yum. Better than it sounds.

That's our breakfast.

I turn around and we walk quietly toward the south. Following the ancient City Wall.

A conversation starts between us, ping ponging back and forth between the three of us.

Our chatter takes all kinds of forms...

Sometimes we relate events to each other.

We might comment on people or things we pass or see nearby.

Now we're heading east along the City Wall.

Passing the South Gate, groups of tourists posing for photos have to be dodged and walked between.

Further on, my buddy becomes excited to show me something he's discovered.

He scampers up a grassy dirt path.

I follow him, huffing and puffing.

We reach the top, a wide area something like the top of a dike, broad enough for a cart or vehicle to ride along.

Up and down the path we can see old stones and bits of brick...part of the original City Wall?

Turning around to face the west, as far as we can see, the mountains sprawl before us.

A spectacular view.

Off in the distance I see the university tucked into the mountains.

A little further on, a major landmark, a hulking hotel overlooks the city.

A few other buildings I hadn't noticed before.

To our right, several pagodas, said to have been constructed during the days of an important kingdom centered in this valley some 1,000 years ago.

Coming down off the wall, we see that the town is coming to life.

Businessmen walk swiftly past us.

Old women in colorful blue and red traditional dress, headed with their loads to the market or the fields.

Children in uniforms on their way to school.

We stop to chat with a language teacher and then move on.

Elderly couples out for an early morning stroll.

Our conversation ebbs and flows, moving from family members, work concerns, comments on the people we pass, other folks we know in town...

Nearly two hours pass.

My feel are feeling tired, and we are coming back around to our starting point.

We say a quick goodbye, and my friend heads up the hill to repair his fence.

I move off in the other direction toward town, looking for 2,500.

A special time spent at the start of a day.

March 29, 2012

Prayer walk with Dave Jacob

HONG KONG NIGHT

The clouds hang heavy over the harbor
Strolling the rocky beach at dusk
Shades of gray meet our eyes
A fresh breeze runs in off the water
Clear ocean waves lap quietly at the rocks
In the distance green hills, now gray, rise out of the
murky waters
Two lights on the horizon suggest lonely fishermen
The clouds hang heavy
A cool moist night in the New Territories.
April 4, 2012

SADNESS

The rooster crowed at seven
As it does
Cool dawn air filters in through the screen
Birds sing happily to the early morn
And my heart hangs heavy
Weighed by sadness
Tears fall within me.
I remember the suspenders
The everyday yellow ones
His gaunt cheeks and sweet lisp
Sitting up in bed in his tiny room in Sheffield
Lost with the Hardy Boys
Then he's grown up
Music, guitars, Scott Joplin, Chinese food
Cycling Er Hai Lake
Out late with his Chinese friends
His farewell concert
Too soon he's leaving us
Johnny is gone
My heart is hanging very heavy.
April 22, 2012
For MPC...for her inspiration to me

A MARVEL

Marvelous what our father did for us undeserving
Do we realize?
Do we marvel?
Do we yawn?
Do we hedge?
Do we hold on?
Do we really, in fact, believe?
If someone is dying...
Do I help him now...or wait for the right moment?
Till I'm ready...till it's convenient...till it's not so costly?
Do I realize that many are dying?
Am I interested?
Do I care?
If I possess the tools to help...or rescue...what will I do?
Wait for the perfect timing?
Till I feel like it?
Till my hands won't get dirty?
What a marvel...
My father didn't wait to help me...
So why am I?
April 28, 2012

I BELIEVE

What does it mean to believe?
Paul wrote to the Romans,
"If the way you live isn't consistent with what you believe, then it's wrong."
What we hold dear is based on belief.
Yet what does it mean to believe?
Is it words?
Saying I agree with or acknowledge an idea?
Paul maintains that how we live determines whether our belief is valid.
So if I say I believe the Message, it must change my behavior.
It will affect how I live my life.
If God wants everyone to know him, and wants us to be about doing that,
Should it not concern and burden me as well?
May 6, 2012

THE VALUE OF LIFE

Who can place a value on life...
Can life be measured by one's intelligence?
By one's beauty?
Personality?
Potential to contribute or produce?
The amount of effort needed to care for a person?
Is there some measurement that will tell us who is of value?
Or, perhaps, after all, the value of a life should be let in the hands of the One who gives life...
May 11, 2012

THEY COME

Giggling girls
Holding pastel parasols
Skip up the walkway
Bending down
They remove their tiny
Colorful Converses
Smiling and chattering
They spill into our living room
Eagerness and excitement
Written on their faces
They love to come
They tell us
And we love their visits
Like sponges
They soak up our discussions
Reading, talking, and asking questions
They drain us
We fall into bed
Worn out and deeply satisfied
And we wonder that
More don't want to share
This privilege.
June 13, 2012

THE CARD

A card
Fell out of the book
A book
Sent in a package
From a friend across the ocean
Picking up a children's book
I opened it
And the card slipped out
Curious, this card
Was it an accident
Where did it come from
A shiver rose up my spine
Into my chest
As I listened to her
Explain the Message on the card
To the gals with us
A complex character
Was printed on the card
A complicated Chinese character
She asked the girls
What the character means
They knew
Combining two words
The character is composed of a
Lamb on top and
Me underneath
Together, Lamb over me
Becomes the word righteousness

The girls caught their breaths and gasped
Having recently heard the story
Of the Lamb providing me righteousness
They understood the significance
Where did this card come from
How did the character originate
Something of a mystery.
June 19, 2012
Dedicated to Brennan Lequire, who sent us the books

WITH THE FAMILY

David whistling as he finishes up the dishes…
Peter's slender fingers working their magic on a gentle melody by Frederic Chopin…
Carrie quietly tending to her studies…
Elsbeth resting while perusing a book…
And I am taking in the majesty and greatness of three of the most wonderful and beautiful prayers even penned…King David's Psalms 103, 139, and 145.
What amazing words.
June 27, 2012

SUCH TENDERNESS

With deep tenderness
You talk to us
With words so precious
You describe us
With such grace
You pour out your affection on us
With the most beautiful worlds ever penned
You whisper to us, your treasure
Your words never cease to amaze me
How can they be true
*Your unfailing love toward those…
Is as great as the height of the heavens
*Your love remains forever
*You place your hand of blessing on my head
*I can never get away from your presence…
Your strength will support me.
*How precious are your thoughts about me…
I can't even count them.
*Filled with unfailing love…
He showers compassion on all
*He is gracious in all
*You satisfy the hunger and thirst
Of every living thing.
*He is filled with kindness.
*Close to all who call
This is what you think of us
This is how you love us
So why…

Why is it that we are not the same
Toward those you love
Behaving callously
Living indifferently
Concerned only for ourselves
Teach us, show us, help us
To love as you love
To care as deeply as you do
To live as you would want us to live.
July 21, 2012
Quotes from Psalms 103, 139, 145 (NLT)

QUESTIONS AND COMMENTS

It's all a fairytale, right?

When will it start talking about America's history?

Will I become good then?

How can I find the right person to marry?

Can I ever be forgiven?

Does he love Americans the most since he made them so rich?

(LC: I think he loves the Chinese the most since he made so many of them!)

I thought all Westerners believed.

How could they have problems if they both believe?

I'll treasure this with all my heart.

My boyfriend and I are going away together for the weekend.

I read some, but it's too hard to understand.

I believe it, too.

No, thanks, I'm not interested right now.

What is this saying to me?

Why did they kill everyone?

I think I need to believe.

My roommates told me I've changed since I started reading.

Now I believe in him.

I wish I had never met you so I wouldn't have to think about all these things.

I feel confused about all these things I've been thinking about.

Sometimes I don't think I'm sitting on the fence

anymore.

You're teaching fish to swim (after studying the meanings of some Chinese characters).

He seemed too harsh in his punishment.

Mom, you need to believe, too.

Will he receive me before I receive him?

We are stunned by what he endured.

You are his gift to me.

You are the bridge to him for me.

I feel like a lost bird who has found a home.

I can't understand why you would come here.

I love coming to see you.

July 23, 2012

THE TOOLS HE HAS GIVEN US

1. God's Message and a love for it
2. Love for China and the Chinese
3. Biblical education and understanding
4. Our family to share with the Chinese

LOVING OTHERS

Is it kindness and love to accept others' beliefs as equally legitimate and meritorious? Is it kindness and love for one with cancer, and who has the cure, to accept the ineffective cures of nine other cancer sufferers as equally legitimate and meritorious instead of sharing with them the effective cure?
September 9, 2012

LOVING THE WORLD

Is it loving the world - according to God's Message - to care for ourselves primarily, to protect ourselves, to focus primarily on protecting our own prosperity?
When did Jesus do that?
When did Paul do that?
September 9, 2012

HEAVY

Lord, my heart is heavy…sad
You of course know me and know why
But I need to tell you
I need to share my tears
My sad heart with you
The suffering and pain weigh heavy
Like a ton of rocks on my shoulders
Or a dagger in my chest
Why Lord?
Is this necessary?
Why this suffering that pierces others?
Lord, come clear away the messes.
Fix wrongs…
Clean up the dirt.
Lord, come.
Wake us up.
Humble us.
Bring us low where it's needed.
Lord, let justice prevail.
Cut out our dross and rot.
Hold on to us and don't let us go.
We hope in you.
We look to you.
We wait for you.
Thank you for your promises.
Thank you that you won't abandon us.
September 20, 2012

SAFE

Giving someone the gift of feeling safe with you...is an important aspect of love and friendship.
October 7, 2012

KINDNESS

Kindness is an essential ingredient in marriage. Those who are not aware of this...may find that they are not in a happy marriage.
October 30, 2012

GOOD QUESTIONS

Why don't I feel as excited as I did last summer?
How do we know the Bible is really true?
Why don't more people believe?
What does it mean to seek first his kingdom?
November 1, 2012
Jason, Christine, Pancho

POLITICS

Slaves bought and sold,
Gladiators thrown to the lions,
Emperors killing their own family members,
Emperors ordering political opponents to kill
themselves,
Harsh religious persecution,
And other gruesome acts too horrible to mention...
Such was life in the Roman Empire.
Why were the writers of the Good Book silent about
all this,
Given that all this was taking place during the same
period?
Why during this national election are believers so
preoccupied with the outcome?
Have we slipped into the very same error that the
Jews succumbed to in Jesus' day - looking for a
political solution or deliverance?
I'm inclined to believe so...
"So we fix our eyes not on what is seen, but on what
is unseen,
since what is seen is temporary, but what is unseen
is eternal."
2 Corinthians 4:18 (NIV)
November 7, 2012

PERSEVERANCE

While Noah labored for 100 years to build the ark, not one of his neighbors believed his Message from God. But he persevered in obeying God's improbable Message.
November 13, 2012

SERIOUS

How seriously do I consider my own sins?
Any of them was enough to send Christ to the cross.
November 17, 2012

CHOSEN

Almost unique among Bible characters, Paul's understanding that he was chosen is what drove and motivated him - even in the midst of suffering, persecution, and disappointment.

Most of the people in the Bible narrative - Moses, Joseph, Job, David, Elijah, Samson, Saul, Peter, Ezekiel, Hosea, Gideon - were reluctant participants much of the time. But knowing he had been chosen, and keeping that understanding in the forefront of his mind, allowed him to endure all sorts of hardship, persecution, and suffering...and to do so with joy...because he knew he was where God had chosen him to be.

"My life is worth nothing unless I use it for doing the work assigned me by the Lord Jesus - the work of telling others the Good News about God's wonderful kindness and love." Acts 20:24 (NLT)

Spoken by Paul to the leaders of the church at Ephesus.

Lord, keep this in the forefront of my mind as well.

"This letter is from Paul, chosen by God to be an apostle." Ephesians 1:1 (NLT)

November 19, 2012

PAUL

Paul's lifestyle must have taken him around the bend...
I mean, who in his right mind, writing to his friends from prison,
Following opposition, beatings, and abuse,
would have only been full of praise to God for his goodness and love
(As he talks about to his friends in Ephesus)?
I mean, really, think of all the things we have to complain about...
November 21, 2012

VISION

"I was chosen to explain to everyone this mysterious plan…" Ephesians 3:9 (NLT)

Limited vision was decidedly not one of Paul's faults. Even as he sat in a dark, dirty dungeon, he was certain that God had assigned him the task of telling everyone!

What a crazy guy!

How crazy am I?

November 22, 2012

REST

"Keep the Sabbath days holy, for they are a sign to remind you that I am the Lord your God." Ezekiel 20:20 (NLT)

God gave us days of rest so that our attention would be kept focused on him. We need this!

November 27, 2012

ATTENTION

"I might fill them with horror so they would know that I am the Lord." Ezekiel 20:26 (NIV)

God gives me hard circumstances when I need my attention turned back to him - so I can thank him for these difficulties which are for my good.

November 27, 2012

VALUE

"I consider everything a loss because of the surpassing worth of knowing Christ." Philippians 3:8 (NIV)
Is this me? Is this my life?
November 27, 2012

WORRY

"Do not be anxious about anything." Philippians 4:6
(NIV)
Is this really possible? Can I really do this? Only if I
do what Paul tells us to do in Colossians 3:1 "Set your
sights on the realities of heaven." (NLT)
November 27, 2012

LIFE IS LEARNED

"I have learned to be content." Philippines 4:11 (NIV)
Even with all his vast wealth of understanding, Paul
learned...and had to learn...the Christian life...by
living it.
November 27, 2012

TREASURE

"Christ, in whom are hidden all the treasures of wisdom and knowledge." Colossians 2:3 (NIV)
Your greatest treasure, Holy Lord, reserved for us, those who are most undeserving and forever turning from you.
November 27, 2012

ABOVE

"Set your hearts on things above." Colossians 3:1 (NIV)
Surely, Lord, this is the key to true joy and contentment. All that we see and experience down here leaves us somewhat unfulfilled.
November 27, 2012

MP

Once it was impossibly old, ancient and unattainable.

But now it has come.

This girl I knew, who wore jeans and short hair.

Forever wanting adventure, she was never boring.

Looking out for me, I enjoyed being with her.

Kind and thoughtful of others, I always felt welcomed by her.

Though apart, we went through much of life together.

I've always been thankful for this girl.

It seems impossible...but my sister has arrived at 60.

HB, MP

November 28, 2012

LISTENING

"But my heart trembles at your Word." Psalm 119:161 (NIV)
What does my heart listen to?
What is it that gets my attention?
Is this really true for me?
November 28, 2012

PRAISE AND PEACE

"Seven times a day I praise you...
Great peace have those who love your law." Psalm 119:164-165 (NIV)
Am I thinking of, thankful for, giving praise to God...all through my day?
Peace comes to me in knowing that God and the Message he has given us are secure and certain, fixed in the heavens.
November 28, 2012

OTHERWORLDLY

"Devote yourselves to prayer, being watchful and thankful...that God may open a door." Colossians 4:2-3 (NIV)

Paul, are you crazy?

How really can you be watching for opportunities when you are chained in a dungeon?

Thankful?

Devoted to praying?

Paul, you are otherworldly...there was no way you could be thinking of your own self in the here and now.

2 Corinthians 4:18 comes to mind - your whole being was focused on other things.

What a treasure and gift you are to us, Saint Paul!

You who were least and last...

November 28, 2012

NEVER TIRE

White clouds rise and swirl
In the early morning
I lift my eyes to the soaring mountain
As the sun first greets it
In the chilly hours of the day
Watching the day awake
I never, never tire of the sight
At the appointed minute
I hurry to the front window that opens to the west
It is dark and still
In a fleeting instant
Mists above the dark line of the mountains
Burst pink
And come alive
They start their upward dance and swirl
Straining to reach up over the mountain
But on the other side
Something must be pulling them back
The clouds can't break free
They remain tied to the top of the mountain
Then I'm called to breakfast.
November 29, 2012

PAUL SUFFERS

I have worked much harder
In prison more frequently
Flogged more severely
Exposed to death again and again
Five times…forty lashes
Three times…beaten
Stoned
Three times shipwrecked
A night…in the open sea
Constantly on the move
In danger from rivers
In danger from bandits
In danger from my own countrymen
In danger from Gentiles
In danger in the city
In danger in the country
In danger at sea
In danger from false brothers
without sleep
Hunger and thirst
Without food
Cold and naked
Pressure of my concern for all the churches
My grace is sufficient
I delight in weaknesses, in insults, in hardships, in
persecutions, in difficulties.
For when I am weak, then I am strong.
2 Corinthians 11, 12 (NIV)

Paul was the most focused of believers.
Nothing distracted him.
Lord, keep me focused on you as Paul was.
December 7, 2012

PAUL'S ASTOUNDING STATEMENTS

Jesus Christ's slave, chose to be sent out. Romans 1
I can never stop thanking God. 1 Corinthians 1
My gracious favor is all you need. 2 Corinthians 12
My interest in this world died long ago. Galatians 6
As slaves of Christ, do the will of God with all your heart. Ephesians 6
Everything that has happened to me here has helped to spread the Good News. Philippians 1
For to me, living is for Christ. Philippians 1
My life is worth nothing unless I use it for doing...
the work of telling others the Good News about God's wonderful kindness and love. Acts 20
(NLT)
December 16, 2012

LOVE THE LORD

"Love the Lord your God with all..." Mark 12:30
(NIV)
If I am really going to love God with everything I
am and have...it will require a full time effort for the
rest of my days.
August 12, 2013

LOVE YOUR NEIGHBOR

"Love your neighbor as yourself." Matthew 22 (NLT)
If there was one thing I would want...only one thing
I could have...it would be to know God. If I love my
neighbor as myself, should I not also want him to
know God's Message?
September 16, 2013

THE SICK

"Healthy people don't need a doctor - sick people do."
Matthew 9 (NLT)
Who am I spending my life with - the spiritually healthy...or the spiritually sick?
September 26, 2013

THE APOSTLES

(X = 12 disciples)
XPhilip - stoned, Phrygia, A.D. 54
Barnabas - burned, Cyprus, 64
XPeter - crucified, Rome, 69
Paul - beheaded, Rome, 69
XAndrew - crucified, Achaea, 70
XMatthew - beheaded, Ethiopia, 70
Luke - hanged, Greece, 93
XThomas - speared, India, 70
Mark - dragged, Alexandria, 64
XJames the Less - clubbed, Jerusalem, 63
XJohn - abandoned, Isle of Patmos, 63
XJames - beheaded, Judea, 44
XNathanael (Bartholomew) - crucified, Armenia, 70
XSimon the Zealot - crucified, Syria, 74
XJudas (Thaddeus) - beaten, Mesopotamia, 72
XMatthias - crucified, Ethiopia, 70

PRIVILEGE

Lord, what a privilege it was today to study the Ten Commandments with Harry. To talk about your holiness, our inability, your Good News... Lord, how can you entrust such a pearl of great price, such truth of inestimable value...to such weak and sinful fools as we are? Your ways seem incomprehensible, foolish to us...counter to our understanding of wisdom and knowledge. But you will share your glory with no one. You will ensure that your purposes come to pass. So this, indeed, is how your Great News goes into the world...through us unqualified sinners. And your desire is that not one will perish...that no one will be separated from you. Lord, as long as I have strength, as long as I have life...may this also be my desire, my passion, my food and drink. May I spend the remaining time you give me here on this earth sharing the Message with those who have not been privileged to hear it before.
October 2013

PAUL'S DESIRE

"In the hope that I may somehow arouse my own people to envy and save some of them." Romans 11 (NIV)

Paul also struggled to get people interested. Why, Lord, aren't more of your people concerned about the many who've never heard?

October 29, 2013

JEREMIAH

"Jeremiah the prophet said: For twenty-three years the word of the Lord has come to me and I have spoken to you again and again, but you have not listened." Jeremiah 25 (NIV)

Jeremiah...the prophet of persistence and perseverance...

October 31, 2013

NO FEAR

"The righteous will never be shaken. They will have no fear of bad news; their hearts are steadfast, trusting in the Lord. They have scattered abroad their gifts to the poor." Psalm 112 (NIV)

Lord, I am trusting in you and scattering your Message to the spiritually impoverished. Establish the work of my hands.

November 1, 2013

BEAUTIFUL WOMAN

Ebullient with vigor
Spilling with energy
May came into our lives.
Curious, alive, honest, and vocal
She meets us face to face.
She keeps coming
Ever surprising
Ever eager
Embracing an insatiable hunger for life.
Our May.
We love her.
A beautiful woman.
November 1, 2013

PAUL'S PERSPECTIVE

"We are fools for Christ. We are weak. We are dishonored. We go hungry and thirsty. We are brutally treated. We are homeless. We work hard. We are cursed. We are persecuted. We are slandered. We have become the scum of the earth, the garbage of the world." 1 Corinthians 4 (NIV)

Paul was living for eternity, not for this life.

November 3, 2013

LOVING YOUR SPOUSE

You don't have to love your spouse…
Course, if you do choose to love them…
It makes life…
Easier
More enjoyable
Richer
More pleasant
More rewarding
More satisfying
More wonderful
More filled with love
Deeper
More effective
More filled with joy
Less filled with loneliness
Less filled with regret
Less filled with bitterness
Less filled with anger
Less filled with pride…
But the choice is yours…
Today and every day.
I choose love.
February 21, 2014

GOD SPEAKS

A freight train approaching out my window
The wind comes howling, raging
Spring leaves hanging on for dear life
Young saplings bent hard over
God is speaking…
Are we listening?
April 16, 2014

JUDGING

Matthew 7:1-2

Do not judge, so that you won't be judged. For with the judgment you use, you will be judged. (CSB)

Stop judging others, and you will not be judged. For others will treat you as you treat them. (NLT)

Don't condemn others, and God will not condemn you. God will be as hard on you as you are on others! (CEV)

Don't pick on people, jump on their failures, criticize their faults - unless, of course, you want the same treatment. (Message)

Lord, what a profound, habitual, consistent, daily failure I have been at obeying this command. Chisel this out of me and reform me to reflect who you are.

June 18, 2014

THOUGH YOU ARE NO LONGER HERE

Mom, Dad, how I would love to sit with you for an hour or two with a cup of coffee.
But you're not here.
Just to see you once again, to look into your face, to see your soft smiles.
But you're not here.
To share with you our family...what we've been doing, what has been happening.
But you're not here.
To sit quietly and listen to you reflect about life, to hear about your experiences.
But you're not here.
To hear you talk about growing up in China, tasting the Great Depression, living through World War 2, losing two children, feeling the sting of opposition.
But you're not here.
When you were here, you asked us to come visit, to stay a while, to hang around a little longer.
But my life was too busy, too important, too urgent.
Now you're not here.
As kids we so easily wrote you off, criticized you, judged you, even scoffed.
Now you're not here.
How could I have been so blind, so deaf, so foolish?
In my untested and ignorant wisdom, I knew better.
Now you're not here.

I had life all figured out at an unusually early age.
I didn't need your dated, traditional, awkward ideas
to teach me.
Now you're not here.
And now, approaching the twilight of my own life,
I'm finally seeing, hearing, learning.
You were amazing.
Courageous.
Real.
Beyond compassionate.
Fools in this self-seeking world.
Sterling in the life you lived.
Never too important for others.
Gracious in suffering.
Thankful in trials.
Silent before puffed up kids.
Sacrificial in marriage and life.
Teachers in how you lived.
Examples that breathed truth into my own life.
How I miss you!
Just to again have a moment in your presence.
To be able to thank you, admire you, listen - really
listen - to you, to appreciate - in your presence - all
that I have received from and been blessed by you.
But the moments came and passed.
Moments that seemed long, plentiful, available.
But now they are no more.
How I miss you, long for you!
But you're no longer here.
Thank you for the life you lived.
Your righteousness, your compassion, your faith,

your kindness, your grace, your legacy in our lives.
How thankful I am for you, though you are no
longer here.
August 8, 2014

DEAR WIM, PHILIP, AND JONATHAN,

How I do miss my big boys and often wonder how you all are doing and what is happening in your lives. Probably the hardest thing about growing old is that, bit by bit, your family is dismantled and taken away from you. That special unit that you have poured your life into and that is your most special treasure, starts to walk right out the door, one by one, never to return as you knew it before. Wow, that is painful. I got plenty of warning about gray hair and various aches and pains that come with old age, but those are child's play compared to losing your family little by little. I do know, from the occasional photo, that JH is having a ball as usual. And as long as Philip's in town at the same time as a certain other, he also seems to be OK. With Wim, I'm never sure. He sends the occasional odd picture of one of his kids in various degrees of distress...but what am I to make of that?? Oh well, I guess no loud cry for help must be good news. I remember when I was the last one home in Korea, after Uncle David left for college. I seem to remember a few more laughs and an extra spring in his step from Granddaddy. I realize now that it was not due to him having yours truly all to himself. It was simply that he was slowly beginning to rise out of the heavy responsibilities that weighed heavy on him for so many years. Suddenly, he could laugh and joke again. It seemed that he more easily related to me. Those were special days...that evaporated all too quickly. Well, now I am in the exact same place he was back then. In 8-9 months, Peter will walk out of here, never to return in the same capacity. I am already feeling pain just thinking about that. And then we will only be left with David, and a few months left with him will also disappear like a storm in the night. But I must say, I really have enjoyed these last couple of years with P&D...and I think back on those last years I had at home with my Dad. It just seems easier to enjoy them now that it's only the two of them. The heavy responsibilities of family and work are slowly lifting, and I am beginning to feel like I can again see daylight, enjoy goofing around with them in a way perhaps that I have not done since Wim was little and about the only one at home. Mom and I can enjoy each other more...take a walk together, sit and read a book together, laugh together. Life does have a lot of twists and turns and ups and downs. Unfortunately, we always want and expect life to be fair...to be equal to all. If there is one thing I have seen loud and clear as I've been interviewing elderly Chinese on the streets here in Dali, it's that life certainly does not deal each of us a fair hand. Many of them were only dealt a two of clubs. By comparison, you and I were dealt three full decks, with the opportunity to play any card at any time. Alllll that to say, looking back, it pains me also to realize that as we passed through life, each of our kids was not dealt the same hand in the family journey. No doubt about it...Wim, Peter, and David got the best hands in terms of what Mom and I could offer them. When Philip was in his critical growing up years, I had heavy work responsibilities, Mom had a potentially terminal illness, and I had crippling depression. We just were not there for you, Phil, and perhaps for one or two of the others as well. I talked with you about this before, and I feel great pain about it as I look back and see the years that cannot be recovered, both as a family, and in terms of my relationship with you. Some things in life are very hard...but there's no way to turn back the clock. But I hope all three of you will remember this experience of mine. Because one day a time like this may come for you. These times usually rear their ugly heads in our 40s, when we have heavy work responsibilities, teens at home, and parents beginning to need our help. At times, it all seems too heavy for us, and we feel we just can't cope. I remember many days in Sheffield, coming home from work, going into my bedroom, and just shutting the door. With everything else weighing on me, I just had nothing else to give to the family. I hope you won't experience something like this. But very likely, some of you will. So I guess I just want to give you a heads up in case the pressure comes on you in this way at some point. I didn't fully realize what had happened and was happening until maybe 10 years later, so I could finally talk about it with Wim and Philip. Some things really seem out of our control and perhaps beyond our ability to cope with. You may experience a few years which later you will look back on as having lost. I would just encourage you to try to be alert to a time like that, and when later you are up to it, try to express and convey to your kids a little of what you were going through, what the family dynamics were, and perhaps that you are sorry to have not been all the way there for some of your kids. I do feel really sorry and sad both for you and for myself, that I missed some key years, for some of you when things were especially heavy for Mom and me. One Chinese man I interviewed this week said he couldn't even talk about his parents and grandparents because when he even thought about them, it brought him to tears, their lives were so hard. Life really doesn't always deal us a fair hand as we wish it would, and I am especially sad for the kids who did not receive our best family years. Sure love each of you guys and want you each to have wonderful lives serving our Father.

Dad

August 29, 2014

PHILIP

Thanks for sharing your heart, Dad. And for being willing to be vulnerable and open with us, and with me in particular. Hard for me to not get emotional and cry when I read this - in part because it was hard growing up the way we did, away from our home culture, without many consistent and close friends, with Mom sick with cancer, with you depressed and absent, and with a lot of other siblings vying for the same attention I needed and wanted...but more so because I can't often find the words to communicate to you how proud I am to call you my Dad, how much I respect the way you have sacrificed everything for your family and for others, how you have chosen to do what's challenging and hard for the chance that others might get to know and see Jesus...I am proud of you, Dad. And I deeply love and respect you. You have consistently and faithfully lived a life in service of God and others. I love you, Dad. So much. Really miss having you close these days.

Phil

September 1, 2014

SURELY

Surely,
Lord God Almighty, eternal Creator of the universe,
Surely,
The greatest gift we could receive from you is the privilege to live with you for eternity.
Gone forever will be ignorance, hatred, poverty, tears, sickness, pain, loss, heartache...
Surely,
This will be the most precious treasure any living human can imagine receiving.
Surely,
Such a priceless treasure could not be trusted to be handled by mere fallible earthly beings.
The angels in heaven rejoice greatly when even one unknown soul enters into your majestic presence.
Surely,
This occurrence dwarfs any other event on earth.
Surely,
How unfathomable, then, how beyond understanding or comprehending, how beyond any measure of reason or reasonableness...that you would, in fact, offer us that exceedingly inconceivable privilege, blessing, and honor to actually be entrusted with the greatest Message in history, in the universe...that Message that opens the way for anyone to spend forever with you, in your perfect presence.
Surely,

This is beyond our ability to understand...
Surely,
As much as anything else, this trust you bestow on us communicates your great, deep love for us...that you would allow us, offer to us, the honor and gift of handling that greatest, most valuable of Messages from you, the Highest Being, to each living being.
Surely,
Your love and your ways are beyond what we can begin to absorb and imagine. Heavenly Father, may we never make light of this honor of honors, privilege of privileges, blessing of blessings that you place in our weak and fragile hands.
October 27, 2014

WHAT DO WE SEE?

Looking around us, what do we see?

Across the oceans, beyond our borders, what do we see?

Silent plagues, fearsome killers scorching our world.

Hatred within humanity, spilling out in holocaust.

Raging, blind fury, razing and butchering everyone in its path.

All our knowledge, advances, power, and greatness...

Flattened by these ancient horrors.

Unstoppable destruction, revealing our smallness and frailty.

This is what we see, Lord, this is what we see...and we tremble in fear.

Death marching toward us, destroying our world.

Fright and fear growing, courage and confidence crumbling.

And we wonder...what do you see?

What do you see, Lord, when you look at this world?

Your perspective and viewpoint are radically different from ours.

What do you see that we don't see?

Aren't you concerned that our living place, this world, is being shaken and torn to pieces?

So, what is it that you see?

This is what you tell us...

You are in control in spite of how things look to us.

The Lord reigns. Psalm 93 (NIV)

What is visibly happening around us is not what is most important.

So fix our eyes not on what is seen, but on what is unseen.

For what is seen is temporary, but what is unseen is eternal. 2 Corinthians 4:18 (NIV)

The terror and evil we see are not the whole story or the final word.

Give thanks to the Lord, for he is good. Psalm 106 (NIV)

I will sing of your love and justice. Psalm 101 (NIV)

All that we see gives us fear and uncertainty.

All that you see is adequate to give us great reason to be joyful, thankful, and at peace.

Come, let us sing for joy to the Lord. Psalm 95 (NIV)

Give thanks to the Lord. Psalm 105 (NIV)

Lord, help us to see through your eyes.

October 29, 2014

THIS GIRL

From before time I planned you.
In my mind I put together this precious girl.
Then I formed her.
Her soul, her mind, her body, her character.
I formed them all, perfectly as I wanted her to be.
Into her body, I breathed life.
Not only breath, but I offered her life to live.
This life I gave her, I wanted her to use...
Spending it to know me, to experience joy, to enjoy my world.
I sent her my Message, so she would know me.
So she would know my deep, everlasting love for her.
Then I sent friends to help her understand my Message.
And now I wait...
Wait to know this girl more fully, for her to know me.
For this precious girl, XiuXiu, Mona, for this girl I patiently wait.
Until the day she chooses to have a relationship with me.
Her Heavenly Father.
November 9, 2017
Written for Mona...
Lewis C.

HEAVY

With my book next to me and one leg tucked under me,
I relax on our reed lounge chair under the living room window.
The winter winds howl, then rush by, stirring up leaves and banging the front gate.
My heart is heavy.
I look at the majestic Himalayas rising up to the heavens above us.
Snow streaks down the crevices and gullies of the Cang Shan.
A few weak clouds pull themselves up over a ridge, a cleft in the line of the mountains.
Every morning, every evening, I look up to the mountains, trying to read the clouds.
A brilliantly sunny day, the clouds are still there, lifting themselves over the ridge line.
I love this view, and my heart is heavy as I look at it now, knowing it will one day only be a memory.
Fifteen years ago, he walked up the hill, along with an orange UT cap on his head.
One last look on that August day as we left our first born at college.
Next week we take our number eight to leave on that same hill this summer, and then we will be left with only our last born with us.
In place of our children, I now feel a heaviness in my heart.

Where did the years go?

Yesterday we struggled to keep our chins above water with all nine at home.

When our first one left, I had no idea that our family would unravel so quickly.

Having our last one left behind doesn't feel like much of a family.

Instead I feel like a death sentence hangs over me.

The kids are grown, and the twilight faces us.

All this life that has been so meaningful to us here will also soon be gone.

Growing old doesn't frighten me, but losing all we've known leaves me with a heaviness in its place.

Even knowing we'll be back soon, my heart is heavy.

Leaving for a few months only reminds me that one day we'll walk away and not come back.

We have been privileged and greatly blessed to be here, and it's painful and sad to think of leaving.

My heart is heavy.

Lewis

February 28, 2015

Dali, China

TWO GIRLS

Up ahead, two blond foreign girls were posing for photo shots of each other.

As we approached, I could pick up their Russian.

"Do you want a shot together?", I asked.

"Oh, yes!"

Taking a couple of semi-candid poses, I chatted for a minute or two.

One was Russian, the other Ukrainian...

"Welcome to Dali!", they said as I waved and headed on down the road.

Moments later I was aware of the New Testament in my pocket and wondered why I had not offered it to them...

Would that be their only opportunity to hear the Greatest News?

It still haunts me.

March 8, 2016

38 SPECIALS

1. You were kind to a shy teenager from Korea.
2. You showed love to the old folks at St. Barnabas Nursing Home.
3. You were enthralled at God's creation.
4. You loved singing the familiar old hymns.
5. You loved entering God's house.
6. You said yes!
7. You cared for a lonely, hungry student during the summers with your letters and breads.
8. You enthusiastically jumped in to building a home and family together.
9. You set aside a promising medical career for your family.
10. You rebelled in small things - weekend getaways, gardening, experimenting in the kitchen, walks together...
11. You were devoted to your parents and family.
12. You appreciated your Dutch heritage.
13. You were diligent in hard things - chopping onions one summer, contributing to a boss and team at DuPont.
14. You were graciously accepting of my parents and family.
15. You were ecstatic to be starting a family together.
16. You enjoyed reading aloud together with

me.

17. You willingly gave up your career and home for me.

18. You happily started again to make a new home for me.

19. You thrived on enlarging the tent stakes of our family.

20. Each child was a treasure to you.

21. You built traditions for our own family.

22. You enthused in visiting my birth and childhood home.

23. You enjoyed praying for, supporting, and reaching out to missionaries.

24. You took up the huge task of educating and training our own children.

25. You were undeterred in raising our children to honor God even without full enthusiastic support from some quarters.

26. You sewed clothing for us.

27. Your occasional weariness was not translated into discontent.

28. You always looked your best and did your best.

29. You were willing to lay aside a career that you loved to follow me into the unknown.

30. You accepted the dismantling of our home and life in order to serve God in a new way.

31. You enthusiastically accepted a spartan life in a distant land with a culture that was foreign to us.

32. You willingly moved again to a new and

different land, being heavily pregnant and knowing no one.

33. You fought courageously and valiantly when your life hung in the balance with cancer, never giving up hope in God.

34. You reached out to other women battling cancer with God's comfort.

35. You released your children from home when that day came.

36. You were always devoted, loyal, and faithful to our family.

37. You never wavered from committing to serving God with your life.

38. You made the decision and commitment and sacrifice to spend your life with me.

"He who finds a wife...receives favor."

"His indescribable gift..."

To Elsbeth

December 16, 2016

38 years together

WILL I?

God, what are you doing?
Can we understand you?
Trust you?
Jesus told us that only you are good.
In the Psalms, we read that your plans will with complete certainty come to pass.
Then Proverbs declares that everything works out according to your own good plans.
But we don't see it, Lord...
Everywhere we look, far and near, the world displays a tragic, miserable mess.
Wickedness, scorn for you, butchery and massacres...
Even we who know you seem too weak, absorbed with ourselves, and incapable of making even the tiniest impression on a world marching deliberately away from and against you.
So we wonder...can we trust you?
Do you really know what you are doing?
Does God really guide the affairs of men, of history...
It seems to us that heaven, which you want filled with all your created beings, may only be scarcely populated.
So much of the world is moving in a direct line away from you...
So we ask...what are you doing?
Where are your good plans that are coming to pass?
Then...in the depths of this quandary, you remind

me of a simple truth that I know already but daily forget.

Like a father to his small child, you are a mystery to us.

We can't begin to understand you or comprehend how and what you do.

But that does not diminish your goodness, your greatness, or the certitude of your plans.

Simply because we cannot understand an infinite God - or his plans - does not mean you are not in control or carrying out your plans.

I just today am not able to see what you are doing.

But I know you can be trusted - that you are trustworthy.

Because I have observed your trustworthiness in all I have seen and experienced, I know that I can also trust you for what I do not see and cannot understand.

So will I trust you?

Yes, I will. And, Lord, help my unbelief.

Lewis

December 21, 2016

IT TAKES TWO

I remember receiving a letter once from my Grandpa. He was writing about the bus or train schedules that he kept up with so well and enjoyed advising people about, long before the advent of computers or the Internet. Grandpa passed on during my freshman year in college. He was 85; I was 18. I can hardly remember a single other word or communication from him during my lifetime, except for when he asked me to go up the driveway and fetch the morning newspaper for him...which I did rather grudgingly, I seem to remember.

It seems that he had very little impact on me. Was his life one long invisible existence? I have wondered as much. Now that I am 60, and have been married close to 40 years, I increasingly realize that I am very much life my Grandpa, and that my life probably appears to others quite a bit as his life seemed to me...a quiet passing across the world stage with very little visible mark left behind.

Was his life really of no consequence? Did his life even matter? And what about my own? It is something I've been pondering, perhaps even with a little unease. Have I done anything with my life? Has it made a difference to anyone?

I don't really know. At this point, it may be a little late for me to be considering these questions. After all, my most productive season of life is passing (or has passed), and my direct influence on my own children is largely over.

But it is a concern to me - if for no other reason than that I am aware that some of our nine children are (for better or for worse) a lot like me - because I realize that some of our children may face or wrestle with these very same questions during their lifetime.

As I think about it, there are three areas that I have contributed to my family, and I can also see that my Grandpa most surely did to his as well - and that my own children with similar makeups may give to their families some day, too.

They are in the areas of spiritual leadership, financial well being, and marital complementarity.

1. A spiritual compass. My wife has an abundance of energy and intellect, far more than I possess. It has caused me often to think of her as the engine of our family, while I have provided the spiritual direction or compass. (Others may disagree!) Providing spiritual leadership does not mean that one must be a spiritual giant, an eloquent speaker, or an acknowledged leader in the church. It does mean that you are the one who makes sure your family is headed in the right direction - in terms of personal and family spiritual devotion, and in terms of church involvement and ministry direction. Is my family headed in the right direction? What am I doing or

should be doing to ensure that it is?

2. Financial health and harmony. Perhaps in no other area in families are there greater disagreements, battles, and disharmony than in the area of money. I don't recall any problems with money arising in Grandpa's and Nai Nai's home, even though as a pastor and missionary his income was always rather modest. By example and by choice, however, Grandpa ensured that finances did not become an area of division or contention within the family. This has also been the case in our own family. In large part it has been due to Mom's own carefulness with money (thanks to Opa, her own father!) and her seeming lack of need for the finer things in life, that we have always managed comfortably. Our moderate income has always been sufficient, we have always lived within what we earned, we always gave back to God, we considered everything as belonging equally to both of us, and we have never allowed money to become a divisive issue or even a driving issue in what we did with our lives. We have been spared much angst which might otherwise have been there.

3. Marital and family union and unity. Anyone who observed my grandparents' family would have said that Nai Nai was the driver, the decision maker, the determiner

of how the family lived. But was that, in fact, entirely the case? I expect not. And perhaps in my inflated view of myself, I might think the same of our own family. Most people notice Mom, converse with her, and remember her as the influential one in the family. Certainly she is the more social, extrovert, and given to expressing her opinions for the two of us. But the reality is that it takes two to make a marriage and family thrive and remain healthy. Just as her energy and drive are essential, so are my complementing of her, my giving her the space and acceptance to make her contribution vital, and my...dare I say it... graciousness (again, some may disagree!) in receiving her contribution to the family. Mom's gift to the family is serving and giving. But in order for it to be effective and successful in contributing to the well-being of the family, it has to be received and acknowledged with thanksgiving. I suspect that my Grandpa was successful at receiving Nai Nai's energetic contribution with thanksgiving. That provided the oil which made the family engine and unit work so well.

LC

December 21, 2016

This was written especially for our children who

share some of my peculiar character traits, in the hope that understanding ourselves and each other might make the path of life a little more smooth for all of us.